FROM THE BARRIO

A Chicano Anthology

LUIS OMAR SALINAS

LILLIAN FADERMAN

California State University, Fresno

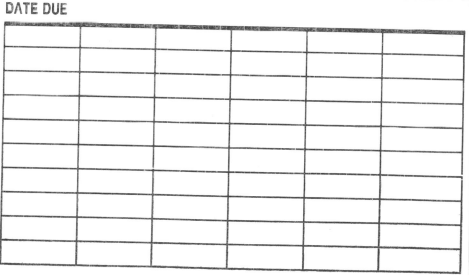

DATE DUE

DEMCO, INC. 38-3012

ɸ CANFIELD PRESS
San Francisco

A Department of Harper & Row, Publishers, Inc.
New York   Evanston   London

From the Barrio: A Chicano Anthology
Copyright © 1973 by Luis Omar Salinas and
Lillian Faderman

International Standard Book Number: 0-06-382639-9
Library of Congress Catalog Card Number: 72-7825

Cover and book design by Joseph M. Roter

73 74 75 10 9 8 7 6 5 4 3 2 1

Contents

Foreword

The poets, fiction writers, and essayists who are collected in this text have one thing in common: they are *Chicanos* concerned with *Chicanismo*, both as a political stance and as a life style. However, the reader will discover within the framework of that common concern a whole spectrum of attitudes, from unrelenting political militancy to placid praise for a *Chicana* lover.

The two-part organization of the book suggests the spectrum: Part I, My Revolution, presents literature that seeks to make a political statement. A multiplicity of attitudes is to be found even within this part—from the bitter anger of Roberto Vargas' poetry to the gentle, bewildered realization of the alienation of all ethnic minorities in America in Leonard Adamé's "Lost Together with Our Children."

Part II, My House, presents literature that seeks to make a personal statement. Sometimes the statement describes life in the *barrio*; sometimes it deals with the experiences of mixing in an Anglo world; sometimes it celebrates *Chicano* beauty; and often it expresses pain or happiness that transcends the ethnic.

Some of the writers whose works appear in this text have been writing for decades and have been published by major American publishing houses. Others have started writing very recently and have been published in the *Chicano* underground papers and magazines. Some have written no more than a dozen poems or three or four short stories and have never been published. But all of them bring to literature a new voice—the *Chicano* voice—which has been neglected by readers and critics for far too long.

Luis Omar Salinas
Lillian Faderman

California State University, Fresno
1972

PART I

MY REVOLUTION

What is the Chicano *revolution? What were the events that gave birth to it and the attitudes that fostered it? Who are the revolutionaries? On what battlegrounds do they fight?*

The Chicano *movement was born in the 1960's, not long after the Black movement for liberation and power. Its rhetoric often has much in common with the rhetoric of the Black movement and with that of movements for liberation of other deprived peoples because the goals of these movements are generally similar: Each desires to maintain integrity while wresting for itself the power and the respect which have hitherto been granted only to a select group and to the very few who learned how to mirror the image of that select group. But despite the similarity of rhetoric with other movements, the* Chicano *movement has developed much that is indigenous to itself. It has developed its own heroes (see "Guevara . . . Guevara," "Ernesto, Emiliano, y Doroteo," and "The Legend of Gregorio Cortez"); and it has learned to re-cast its myths to serve the revolution (see "Chac"). It has learned to define the enemy within and the enemy without (see "To Brothers Dead Crossing the Rápido River . . . 194 . . . ," "They Blamed It on Reds," "In Days of Wine," "'And Man Was Made WORD': Chicano Genesis," "Dos Vatos," and "The Dark Root of a Scream"). And, perhaps even more important, it has learned*

1

to recognize the friend within and the friend without (see "The Woman of La Raza," "Lost Together with Our Children," "Elegy Pa Gringolandia in 13 Cantos," and "Primer Canto").

The selections in this part show how a revolutionary is born and how he grows; what he needs to learn as he is growing and what he needs to unlearn; which allegiances will nourish him and which can destroy him. The writers' styles and tones vary from the reasoned argument of Armando Rendón and the subtle twist of Otero y Herrera to the fury of Vargas and the explicit bitterness of Valdéz. But each writes with a sense of history behind him and a vision before him—and each writes of revolution.

Introduction

ALFREDO CUÉLLAR

The Chicano *Movement*

Mexican American political activity has often been related to social structural factors. Because much of this political activity was possible only after certain structural changes in Mexican American life, there were seldom any real alternatives beyond simple reaction to Anglo pressure. The importance of the *Chicano* movement as an alternative to pressures from the majority society can hardly be overemphasized. It is a distinctively novel development in the Mexican American community. The *Chicano* movement developed in southern California no earlier than 1966, and it is already a sharp new force in the political expression of Mexican Americans throughout the southwest.

The *Chicano* ideology includes a broad definition of political activity. Ironically, such thinking was possible only for a new generation of urbanized and "Anglicized" (that is, assimilated) young Mexican Americans, who were much less burdened by social and class restrictions than their elders were and whose education has exposed them to new ideas.

The exact beginnings of the movement are obscure. There is some evidence that the *Chicano* movement grew out of a group of conferences held at Loyola University in Los Angeles in the summer of 1966. As originally conceived by its Catholic sponsors, the conferences were to create a fairly innocuous youth organization for the middle-class Mexican students attending various colleges throughout California. Very quickly the movement grew beyond the intent or control of its sponsors (Loyola has never been very noted for its interest in Mexican American education) and it drew in yet others, not students and not middle class, who were attracted by the ideology of *chicanismo*. Thus it cannot be understood as a movement limited to the young, to students, or even to urban areas. It must also be understood as including the followers of Reies Tijerina in northern New Mexico and César Chávez' embattled union of striking farm workers in central California. In 1969 Rodolfo (Corky) González was the principal leader and inspiration of the *Chicano* movement in Denver although his

Alfredo Cuéllar, "Perspective on Politics" in Joan W. Moore with Alfredo Cuéllar, *Mexican Americans*, © 1970. Reprinted by permission of Prentice-Hall, Inc., Englewood Cliffs, New Jersey.

interests were mainly in urban civic action. Moreover, "Corky" has organized regional youth conferences and his influence spreads far beyond the local area. No one leader has yet emerged in southern California or in Texas.

As this wide range of activity shows, the *Chicano* movement is extremely heterogeneous, and its elements have different aims and purposes. In this way the movement cuts across social class, regional, and generational lines. Its aims range from traditional forms of social protest to increasingly more radical goals that appear as a sign of an emerging nationalism. It is a social movement, in that it can be described as "pluralistic behavior functioning as an organized mass effort directed toward a change of established folkways or institutions."* The dynamic force of the movement is its ideology— *chicanismo.*

The new ideology is advanced as a challenge to the dominant Anglo beliefs concerning Mexicans as well as to the beliefs of Mexican Americans themselves. Although we have emphasized that students are by no means the only element of the *Chicano* movement, we will reconstruct *chicanismo* primarily as it has been developed among students. Actually, this is only one of several ideological strands but it is the most consistently developed, thus the best illustration of the change from protest to nationalism and a synthesis of the ideology of *chicanismo.*

The first student form of the *Chicano* movement coincided with the development of new student organizations in California universities and colleges in 1966 and 1967. Some of these groups were the United Mexican American Students (UMAS), the Mexican American Student Association (MASA), Mexican American Student Confederation (MASC), and Movimiento Estudiantil Chicano de Aztlán (MECHA). More recently the Mexican American Youth Organization (MAYO) has appeared, with particular strength in Texas. (MAYO is also the name adopted by the new organizations of *Chicanos* in California prisons.) These student groups were at first concerned with a rather narrow range of problems in the field of education, particularly those concerned with increasing the number of Mexican American students in college. To the extent that these student groups were active in the Mexican American community, they were involved with various forms of protest against specific and long-standing grievances, such as police brutality and inferior educational facilities, although other forms of community activity also involved political campaigns.

Chicano student groups thus have never repudiated ordinary forms of political activity, although for them such forms as voting constitute only one

*As defined by Abel, in *Why Hitler Came to Power*, as cited in Martin Oppenheimer, *The Urban Guerilla* (Chicago: Quadrangle Books, 1969), p. 19.

political alternative. Actually, given the wide range of problems facing the Mexican American community, *Chicanos* view conventional forms of political activity as perhaps the least effective. Instead, they favor forms of confrontation as the most effective means to gain access for the traditionally excluded *Chicano*, even though it has, on occasion, led to violence. In general, this conception of politics contrasts sharply with the ideas of more conservative Mexican American leaders, most of whom adhere to very limited and "safe" politics with an emphasis on voting and "working within the system" to gain political leverage. This is not to say that *Chicanos* reject working for social change within the system; as a matter of fact, much recent activity has focussed on bringing about change in the universities and colleges as well as in the public school systems. Nevertheless, whereas the moderates seek to bring major change in American society through nonviolent means, the more militant speak of the need for "revolutionary activity," though they often leave the details and direction of this revolution unspecified. While they admire the life style and aspirations of revolutionary leaders like Ché Guevara, they have thus far made no systematic theoretical connection between the *Chicano* movement and the general literature on revolution. The theoretical underpinnings of the *Chicano* movement thus often lack a strong direction.

And yet, the advent of the *Chicano* movement does represent a revolutionary phenomenon among Mexican Americans. As we shall see, most of the change from traditional forms lies in (or is reflected in) the ideology of *chicanismo*. Basically eclectic, *chicanismo* draws inspiration from outside the United States and outside the Mexican American experience. The Cuban Revolution, for example, exerts some influence, as do the career and ideals of Ché Guevera. For instance, the Brown Berets (a *Chicano* youth group) affect the life style of this revolutionary. Black Power also offers something of a model. Most recently, *Chicanos* have resurrected the Mexican revolutionary tradition.

Basically, however, *chicanismo* focuses on the life experience of the Mexican in the United States. It challenges the belief system of the majority society at the same time that it attempts to reconstruct a new image for Mexican Americans themselves. *Chicanos* assume that along with American Indians and black Americans, Mexicans live in the United States as a conquered people. This idea allows *chicanismo* to explain the evolution of the *Chicano* as essentially conflictful. In each conflictual relationship with Anglos, the Mexicans lost out and were thus forced to live in the poverty and degradation attendant upon those with the status of a conquered people. This is no better illustrated than by the Mexicans' loss of communal and private property. As a result, they had no choice but to work the land for a *patrón* (usually an Anglo, but sometimes a Mexican, who exploited his own people). When the Mexican was thrown off the land, he was forced to become an unattached wage-earner, often a migrant farm worker; or he might migrate to a city, where the exploitation continued. In any event, *chicanismo* emphasizes that the Mexican was transformed into a rootless economic commodity, forced either to depend on migrant farm work or to sell his labor in the urban centers, where his fate depended upon the vicissitudes of the economy. Ironically, indispensable as Mexican labor was for the economic development of the Southwest, the Mexican got little recognition for his contribution and even less benefit from it.

Chicanos therefore see the economic expansion of the Southwest as essentially a dehumanizing process. They also point out that during periods of economic depression in the United States, when the Mexican became "superfluous" and "expensive," Anglo society had no qualms about attempting to eliminate Mexicans from the United States, as in the repatriations of the 1930s. . . . The repatriations are viewed as a conscious attempt to eliminate the *Chicano* from American society.

The thrust of *chicanismo* is not only economic, but also cultural. In many ways, the exploitation and suppression of his culture is what most angers the *Chicano*, who views the attempt to deracinate Mexican culture in the Southwest as the reason why Mexican Americans are disoriented about their culture and often attempt to deny it. The *Chicano* points out that the Anglo himself often views Mexicans with a great degree of ambivalence. Anglos oftentimes take over aspects of "Spanish" (which is really Mexican) culture and at the same time deny it to the Mexican himself. In this fashion Mexicans were denied the development of a more autonomous cultural life, especially as it touches upon Spanish language use, the arts, and so on. (This was done in spite of the agreements made in the signing of the Treaty of Guadalupe Hidalgo. Early drafts of the treaty contained Mexican government efforts to make formal recognition of language rights for Mexicans who chose to remain in the United States after the Mexican War. These provisions were not approved by the U.S. Senate.)

Worse yet, the ideology goes on, the cultural suppression continues to the present day, reinforced by Anglo institutions, particularly the schools. The extreme position (although by no means infrequent) is represented by the fact that Mexican American students in the public schools are corporally punished for using Spanish, their native language. Under these circumstances, it is understandable that the Mexican American student remains ignorant and often ashamed of his past. When the Mexican is mentioned in textbooks, it is in a romanticized and stereotypically Anglicized version of "Spanish culture" that may be congenial to Anglos but is remote and irrelevant to the Mexican American. The *Chicano* considers this type of whitewashed "Spanish" culture particularly galling because he feels that while

Anglos may selectively choose certain motifs from Mexican culture, the person behind the culture, the Mexican himself, is given neither recognition nor respect.

Chicanismo also focuses on race, and in some ways this emphasis constitutes one of the most controversial aspects of *chicanismo*. It is argued that Anglo racism denies the Mexican his ethnicity by making him ashamed of his "Mexican-ness." Mexican ancestry, instead of being a source of pride, becomes a symbol of shame and inferiority. As a consequence, Mexicans spend their lives apologizing or denying their ancestry, to the point that many dislike and resent being called "Mexican," preferring "Spanish American," "Latin," "Latin American," and similar euphemisms. For these reasons, the term *"Chicano"* is now insisted upon by activists as a symbol of the new assertiveness.

Advocates of *chicanismo* therefore hope to reconstruct the Mexican Americans' concept of themselves by appeals to pride of a common history, culture and "race." *Chicanismo* attempts to redefine the Mexicans' identity on the basis not of class, generation, or area of residence but on a unique and shared experience in the United States. This means that appeals for political action, economic progress, and reorientation of cultural identity are cast in terms of the common history, culture, and ethnic background of *la raza*.

Chicano ideologues insist that social advance based on material achievement is, in the final analysis, less important than social advance based on *la raza;* they reject what they call the myth of American individualism. The *Chicano* movement feels that it cannot afford the luxury of individualism; if Mexicans are to confront the problems of their group realistically they must begin to act along collective lines. Hence, the stirrings of a new spirit of what *chicanismo* terms "cultural nationalism" among the Mexican Americans of the Southwest.

Chicanismo has led not only to increased participation in community activities, but also to a heightened and often intense interest in cultural life. *Chicano* poets, playwrights, journalists, and writers of all varieties have suddenly appeared. There are *Chicano* theater groups in several large cities (often known as the *teatro urbano*) and one nationally known and well-travelled group from Delano, California (*El teatro campesino*), which tells the story not only of the striking California farm workers but of *Chicanos* in general. Newspapers and magazines also reflect this desire to disseminate the idea of *chicanismo*. Throughout the Southwest numerous *Chicano* "underground" newspapers and magazines publishing literary materials have emerged. There is even a *Chicano* Press Association, a regional association representing *Chicano* publications from Texas to California. Furthermore, because of the strong base in colleges and universities, a serious and generally successful drive to develop "ethnic studies" programs has appeared, especially in California. As part of the drive to spread the idea of *chicanismo* in education, *Chicanos* place an emphasis on Mexican contributions to American society, thus giving *Chicano* college students a new conception of their past and present.

Chicano student groups share an orientation similar to that of black students, and on occasion they cooperate and support each other on similar demands. (There is more mutual support between black and brown students than between their counterparts at the community level.) The alliance between black and brown students, however, has not been close, harmonious, or continuous. *Chicano* student organizations have not yet been significantly involved with Anglo radical student groups, although these groups sometimes claim their support or claim that they are working for the benefit of *Chicanos*.

THE ECHO OF *CHICANISMO*

How much has this student manifestation of the *Chicano* movement reflected the larger Mexican community? At this writing the ideological reverberations have been considerable, particularly among the young people of college age and including also those in the secondary schools. We must not forget that the Mexican American population is very young. Some counterparts of *Chicano* college militancy have appeared throughout the Southwest in high schools as, for example, among students in Denver, Los Angeles, San Francisco, and many smaller cities.

The demands have often been modest, in most instances no more than for increased counselling services for Mexican American students and other changes in the methods and content of instruction. In some Texas cities and in Denver, Colorado, the student militants further demanded the end of punishment for using Spanish on the school grounds. In most cases the school boards have acceded to this particular demand. But the reaction of the Anglo community has often been fierce. In Los Angeles a school "walkout" by Mexican American students in 1968 resulted in the arrest of 13 alleged leaders for criminal conspiracy. In Denver a sharp reaction by the police resulted in the injury of 17 persons and the arrest of 40. In other areas in the Southwest there have been similar, if less publicized, responses to *Chicano* militancy.

Neither the Anglo reaction nor the rapid spread of *chicanismo* should be taken to mean that a full-blown social movement is in progress among Mexican Americans. In many areas, on the contrary, established Mexican American leaders have dissociated themselves from the *Chicanos*. For instance, a school walkout by Mexican students in Kingsville, Texas, brought an angry denunciation from a Mexican American Congressman from Texas and other community leaders. At the same time, the *Chicano* movement poses a very difficult dilemma for most older Mexican Americans. They sympathize with the goals of *chicanismo*, yet they fear that the radical means used to pursue these ends will undermine their own hard-earned social and economic gains. The Anglo community expects a denunciation of what it considers to be irresponsible acts of these young people. But for the older leaders to oppose the *Chicano* protest might be a slow form of personal political suicide as well as acting to exacerbate divisiveness in the Mexican American community.

In California, *Chicano* student groups have grown rapidly; they have acquired the power to pass on Mexican American faculty appointments in many high schools and colleges. Typically such faculty members are avidly sought to assist with the new ethnic studies programs and centers. Ultimately, though, *Chicano* students are faced by responsibility to the community. These students are aware that the popularity of *chicanismo* among Mexican American students means a major opportunity for the development of an entire new generation of young professionals to carry these ideas back to the Mexican American community.

Beyond the universities there have been other sources of support, some of them quite substantial. Grants and direct organizing assistance have come from American Protestant denominations, notably the National Council of Churches. In 1968 a substantial ($630,000) grant from the Ford Foundation to the Southwest Council of La Raza (headquarters in Phoenix) helped the organization of a number of militant *Chicano* groups. The Southwest Council of La Raza considers itself permanent and accepts money for "*barrio* development" from not only the Ford Foundation but churches, labor groups, and other interested organizations. Both the announced ideals of the council and its membership assure commitment to the ideals of *chicanismo*.

The *Chicano* movement began as a protest. Only later did its dynamics carry it toward an increasing cultural nationalism. The first steps toward social change did not go beyond demands for equality of opportunity for Mexican Americans, which are still being made (by the less militant in the movement). Until recently no Mexican American had tried to define the problems of the community in any terms except those of assimilation. It is precisely these ideas of assimilation and social "adjustment" that the *Chicano* militant rejects. As a new alternative, *chicanismo* represents a conception of an autonomous and self-determining social life for Mexican Americans.

It is interesting that it was not until the 1960s that the *Chicano* leaders emerged to question some of the oldest and most fundamental assumptions of Mexicans in American society. This protest probably would not have been possible in a period of general social calm and stability. That the *Chicano* protest emerged when it did is perhaps due in large part to the emergence of other social groups that also began to question basic notions about American society. But if these other groups feel a sense of alienation in American society, the *Chicano's* alienation is doubly acute. It is not only from American society that he feels alienated; he also feels left out of the mainstream of Mexican history and, simultaneously, he feels a sense of guilt for having "deserted" the homeland. It is this sense of being in two cultures yet belonging to neither (*ni aquí ni allá*) that is the source of his most profound alienation and now, anger. It is against this background that the *Chicano* is attempting with a deep sense of urgency to reconstruct his history, his culture, his sense of identity.

In practical terms the result is increasing radicalization, with which comes a new set of problems. Cultural nationalism has emerged, bringing with it questions that must be answered if the *Chicano* movement is to become a potent force for all Mexican Americans in their diverse circumstances throughout the Southwest and other parts of the United States.

Essays

ARMANDO RENDÓN

How Much Longer . . . The Long Road?

Flat, dust-grey fields, burdened with fruits and vegetables, span to the right and left of Highway 99 in California; fields just like them, but broken more often by trees, spread out along U.S. 83 in south Texas; farmlands swell out over the subtly rounded earth beside Highway 49 in southwestern New Jersey; 99, 83, and 49 are major arteries of America's agricultural industry. To people who follow the crops, they signify miles of cramped, sweat-sticky travel by car or bus, dry swallows of roadside meals, the down in the gut fear of being too late or too early for a job.

How much longer this long road for the migrant farm worker? How many more the years of kneeling and picking down the rows of tomatoes or straw-berries, of bending to the short-handle hoe, of being cheated out of a fair day's wage for a fair day's work, of camping on a river bank or renting a broken-down shack, of pulling your children out of school before they get a chance to really learn or even make a friend?

Daily, the migrant seasonal farm worker suffers the want of physical or material goods and the denial of civil and human rights. Whatever his racial or ethnic origin, the oppressive conditions of farm labor debase him to the level of a stepchild of poverty and discrimination.

The rootlessness of his life and his dependency on external measures of supply and demand which he can neither alter nor understand have made of the migrant field worker a man on the fringe of society. His dominant fear is that he will lose his job, however lowly or poorly paid. Yet, his innermost desire is to settle down, in or out of agricultural labor, for his own and his children's sake. That he cannot really influence the course of his life may constitute the most critical injustice exacted of the farm worker.

How this situation has come about and what the current conditions of farm labor are in America have been well documented. The character of farm labor has altered radically since World War II. Certain problems in the present makeup of the farm workforce owe their existence to the shortage of domestic hands during the war years and the subsequent importation of foreign workers. A more crucial issue—the farm worker's unequal standing

Reprinted with permission from the Summer 1968 *Civil Rights Digest* (Vol. I, No. 2), published quarterly by the U.S. Commission on Civil Rights.

in the organized labor movement—dates back to 1935 when, in the enactment of the Wagner Act (precursor to the Taft-Hartley Act) by the 73rd Congress, agricultural workers were explicitly excluded from the definition of "employee." Since then they have been barred from basic Federal labor law.

The introduction of modern, specialized machines into the fields coupled with the development of new and more efficient farming techniques has created new forces to displace or further undermine the wage-earning potential of the human harvester. Efforts of Federal, State, and local governments—even private church, union, and civic groups—have resulted in some progress over the years in certain areas such as health, housing, education, but too often for varying periods of time and degrees of effectiveness. The inclusion in 1966 of farm laborers under the Fair Labor Standards Act might be of more lasting significance. However, even this legislation affects only 380,000 or one-fourth of the farm workforce, restricts farm workers to a top minimum wage projected for 1969 of $1.30 an hour, and excludes them all from overtime provisions afforded other workers covered by the Act.

The farm worker's situation is complex but generally it can be understood as consisting of three major trends, two within the migrant stream, one in the external development of equitable rights and treatment under law. As to the stream, some individuals are striving to drop out, to learn new job skills, to upgrade their education, to establish a permanent homebase; others will continue or join the stream for seasonal work, preferring the work they know best and rural living to the city, but desiring a better life where they are. Outside the stream, but closely related to it, is the provision through legislation of rules and regulations governing work and wage conditions and other essential services or programs which afford the farm worker, whether he is getting out or remaining in the stream, the same extensions of the law as are due other workers. Given this complex situation, it is apparent that simply raising wages to an arbitrary level which is inherently discriminatory cannot begin to affect realistically and broadly enough the fundamental farm labor issues.

To arrive at any clear conclusions or recommendations for action about so complex an issue is difficult. Where do you start? What are the facts? What insights can be provided the concerned person? The very routes farm workers travel to harvest the Nation's food and fiber provide at least an itinerary for gathering information and placing the issues in perspective.

California's Central Valley is one of America's richest agricultural areas. The State boasts some of the largest farm corporations in the country; its economy is one-third dependent on farming for jobs; its income at farm level annually amounts to more than $4 billion. In such an economic setting the California farm worker would be expected to do relatively better than his counterparts in other States. *Relatively*, this is true: in 1967, hourly farm wage rates were highest in California and Connecticut at $1.62. The average wage rate nationwide for farm workers, however, was $1.33 an hour last year, 40 cents lower than the average for laundry workers, traditionally a low wage group. (Four southeastern States paid fieldworkers an average wage below the $1.00 minimum of 1967.) Work patterns, too, are somewhat more stable since there are many of the seasonal farm workers who move generally within the State or have developed a year-round farm work pattern. Also the opportunities for non-farm or even farm-related jobs are greater in the Golden State. Nevertheless, the California fieldhand is still at the bottom of the social pyramid, short on job skills, basic education, decent housing, and income.

Why is this so in such a valley of plenty? In Delano, a farm town between Bakersfield and Fresno, a farm workers' union and grape growers have been engaged in a crucial economic encounter since September 1965. The United Farm Workers Organizing Committee (UFWOC) has been on strike against major producers of wine grapes during the first two years and most recently against fresh table grape growers. The union is headed by César Chávez, a Mexican American farm worker. During the nearly three years of strikes, there have been several incidents of friction and physical clashes between growers and union members or supporters, unrelenting opposition to the union from many sides, and legal encounters as well. Contracts have been won from nine growers, often at great hardship.

The 1968 Report (No. 1274) of the House Committee on Education and Labor, dealing with Coverage of Agricultural Employees under the National Labor Relations Act (NLRA), noted that "the strike for recognition, with all its disastrous consequences, has largely become a thing of the past—in manufacturing, in transportation, entertainment, publishing, food processing, broadcasting, retailing—in all industries but agriculture. There, the law of the jungle which generally prevailed 33 years ago still exists." The Committee report recalls a strike by 5,000 cottonpickers in Corcoran, California, near Delano, which in 1933 resulted in mass evictions, mass picketing, mass arrests, and the death of two workers when a union meeting was forcibly broken up. "Labor unrest on the farm, to varying degrees, continues to this date—in California, in Texas, in Florida, in Michigan, in Ohio, in Wisconsin, and elsewhere ... And the testimony before this committee indicates that in the absence of law, it takes ugly forms which can harm the employers, the employees, and the community."

The "law of the jungle" described by the committee is due in large measure to the fact, then, that farmers and farm workers are outside the jurisdiction of basic labor law and therefore subject neither to the benefits nor the prohibitions of Taft-Hartley.

It was the first day following an agreement by the Immigration and Naturalization Service of the Department of Justice with the United Farm

Workers to enforce a regulation of the Department of Labor prohibiting immigrant Mexican citizens in the United States with Alien Registration Cards (greencard workers) from being brought into the country as strike-breakers when the Secretary of Labor certified a bonafide labor dispute.

On that Friday, April 26, *la migra*, as the Border Patrol is known throughout the Southwest, performed its usual function of scouting by air for suspected aliens, relaying information to a ground team, then chasing suspects down in the fields by jeep or on foot. Early that morning at a farm road intersection outside Delano, two border patrol officers engaged in a brief and heated exchange with Chávez and Roberto Bustos, a union captain. One officer questioned the two union men, asking for their papers, their names, what their purpose was. Chávez refused to give any information and charged the officers with neglecting their duty in the fields. In an apparent effort to intimidate the two men, the officer asked, "Do you want to get arrested?" Shrugging the ploy aside, Chávez replied, "No, but if you want to arrest me, go ahead." The two officers returned to their car and as they drove off, Chávez called out: "What's your name so I can report you to your boss?" The officer behind the wheel retorted, "I'm not telling you my name if you don't tell me yours."

Later that afternoon, *racimos*, or small groups of union members, were assigned to strategic exits of one of the fields owned by Giumarra Vineyard Corporation, largest of the 24 table grape producers being struck in the Delano area. The *racimos* were to pursue strikebreakers seen leaving the fields for their homes. The "scabs" would later be shamed out of the fields by the union through various means: leaflets, word-of-mouth, and door-to-door marches in towns such as Earlimart, Richgrove, McFarland, all near Delano. The United Farm Workers has also been conducting a nationwide boycott of all California grapes in an effort to force its primary target, Giumarra, to the bargaining table. There have been mass arrests, beatings, and economic intimidation by the growers, the farm workers have alleged and charged in various court suits.

Perhaps the open hostility toward the strikers and the counterreaction of unionization tactics such as the "scab" hunt would persist, but the damaging effects to both sides from the recognition strike and the secondary boycott as well as the physical clashes would be mitigated or entirely obviated by amendment of the NLRA. Efforts in Congress to do this, in House Bill 16014 and Senate Bill 8, however, so far have been stymied, one in the House Rules Committee, the other in the Senate Labor and Public Welfare Committee. If farm workers are included in the basic legislation, coercion by either side would be a prohibited unfair labor practice and when voluntary recognition does not occur, 30 percent of the workforce can demand an officially supervised election to decide whether the union will be the sole bargaining agent for the employees.

Chávez asserts that through the union, the farm worker can achieve economic, health, housing, and education standards equivalent to those of workers in other industries. "It is an error to think of programs; this is not what we're after because taking handouts merely destroys the individual. Programs don't mean anything, education doesn't mean anything, unless you have bread on the table. Migrant workers must be given a chance to form a union. The Government can provide the rules; let the workers do the rest."

Other union members echoed Chávez's thoughts. Waiting under the harsh sun, an old traveler of the migrant road crinkled his eyes as he peered along the glaring roadway. "The union is the only way," he said. "My wife and I have four children and a home in Delano. I am getting too old to travel. The oldest girl is in high school and we hope she will graduate. One of my boys is not doing too well but may make it. But I don't want them to follow me."

The woman resting against a vinebush was telling about the years she had spent among the grapevines. Her fingers were distorted and calloused from the work, her skin dust-brown from the sun. Her joy was a son who, she said, was especially bright and looking forward to college and an engineering career. "It's hard our being on strike because we want to help our son get through college. He's a very smart boy. He's never had to work out here and I hope he never will. There's a chance of him getting a scholarship that will help."

A grizzled, work-creased man, the father of eight children, recalled the eight years he had spent in San Antonio, Texas, in various city-type jobs, some of them good-paying, but that he had returned to farm work and rural life where he felt more at ease. "I had enough of that city life. It's too fast and mean. I like working out in the field. I'm strong and I can do the work. But I think we can have it a little better here in Delano. I liked Chávez and the union from the beginning. I've been in the union since before we started the strike—I walked from here all the way to Sacramento where we had the march two years ago. I think we're doing the right thing to get our rights."

A crucial factor that must be considered in amending the NLRA, of course, is the extent of coverage of farmers under the new legislation. A key criticism and stumbling block to the inclusion of farm workers in NLRA has been the contention that small, family farms might be affected adversely by such a change. In fact, House report No. 1274 anticipates that coverage under the wording of House Bill 16014 would extend only to about 30,000 American farms, "roughly nine-tenths of 1 percent of the 3.2 million farms in America"—only those farms which employed at least 12 employees at a time and paid a wage total of at least $10,000 in the past year according to the proposed amendment.

Given these conditions, the House report added, only 44,000 farms were found to fall within the minimum annual expenditure figure of $10,000 according to the Bureau of the Census, Agriculture Division. This number (1.4 percent of all American farms) in the peak final week of May 1966, employed 622,000 farm workers—60 percent of the 1,083,000 who worked on farms that week.

Under the limitation of 12 or more employees, the total number of farms that might expect to be affected by new legislation, the report stated, falls to 30,000 since "most livestock, dairy, and poultry farms" having an annual wage cost of $10,000 or more probably do not hire a dozen or more hands. The 30,000 farms which would be affected by Taft-Hartley, then, would be the fruit and nut, vegetable and cotton growers, who, in turn, hire the most peak harvest workers and, therefore, expend larger amounts in wages.

It is a fact that the UFWOC has been striking, not the small farmer, but the biggest grape growers in the country. These same producers of the grape, it is significant to note, who can best afford the move, are turning in the direction of eliminating, completely if possible, the hand picker, the hoer, and the gleaner from the fields.

Mechanization, a mounting threat to the agricultural laborer in many areas or crops, is less of a specter to Chávez, however, than the strikebreaker, of whatever variety—domestic, greencard, or illegal alien. "The growers are trying to kill the union by scaring us with talk of mechanization," he stated. He said of a grape harvester being developed at the University of California at Davis that even if the machine is perfected, it will pick only one of 22 kinds of wine grape.

Basically, it could be sensed from Chávez' words and the comments of farm worker after farm worker that to the man who picks the crops, the union or community organization in general is the only way that their lives will be improved, that they will be able to exercise their rights fully. As one of the union captains put it, a key objective of the workers is to make the union a major issue on which everyone will have to take sides, on which no one can be neutral. Literally, to them, the union is a life or death issue.

Along the Río Grande, U.S. 83 runs the gamut of poverty. Appalling conditions of hovel housing, hunger, economic dependence, lack of opportunity, unemployment, injustice are in permanent residence here. Highway 83 is a main artery of the migrant stream flowing from south Texas through New Mexico into Arizona and California or up through the Texas Panhandle into the Rocky Mountain States. Main portions of the migrant population move upward to the Great Lakes Region, the North Central States, and some to Florida.

In the Río Grande Valley, a community movement is groping its way into becoming an independent, self-help organization under the name Colonias del Valle. Its headquarters in San Juan, a small one-street town east of McAllen, operates as the Valley Service Center.

Colonias in this part of the country are small housing developments, subdivisions sold lot by lot to local migrant people who build their own houses or contract with the developer. Many are small, tidy homes but with few if any of the modern conveniences. Most are unfit for the people who live in them because they are usually vermin or rodent infested, offer little protection against weather, and are too small for the number of people they shelter. In colonias such as El Gato and El Rincón, the thatch-roofed *jacal* is common, shacks pieced together with strips of tin, wire, sticks, odds and ends of boards. There are no paved streets here, no street lights, running water, or indoor plumbing. Water must be hauled into the colonia in many cases, because wells pump up a bitter, salty brew. Yet in certain areas, too much water, in a flash flood of the Río Grande, can severely damage crops and communities.

In September 1967, Hurricane Beulah roared into south Texas, killing and maiming people on both sides of the border. The hurricane also devastated fields, churning them into sloughs, wiping out, too, many of the already scarce jobs available to the valley residents. The wage-depressing influx of greencarders into this valley has forced families to seek work as far away as Washington and New York—Beulah turned the economic clamp about the farm worker several more notches. From January 1967 levels, farm jobs fell by about two-thirds in 1968 in Hidalgo County alone.

The fear that dominates the migrant is that of losing a job, of not finding the job available that he had lost your because of mechanization, demise of a farm, or arriving too late for the first good pickings. Here, in south Texas, the fear begins—fear for the few days of hoeing or running a tractor, for the prospect of out-of-state jobs, how soon to leave, where to go, getting a loan in time.

Amador is the father of four children; his wife is pregnant. The cooling system in his pickup truck had needed repairs lately and then for two days the vehicle had been missing, stolen. When it was found, the engine was burned out. The cost to repair the engine, he had learned, was more than he could earn in a month on the road. How could he move out now without transportation? For three years he had been among the more than 86,000 people who had engaged in interstate travel out of Texas, and among 39,000 who had ventured out of only four Río Grande Valley counties: Hidalgo, Starr, Camerón, and Willacy. (Other figures compiled by the Texas Employment Commission and the Texas Bureau of Labor Statistics indicate that in 1966, more than 100,000 families or groups left the State while 129,000 sought farm work within the State.)

The story of Amador can be multiplied with minor alterations thousands of times over. The oldest of six children, he began field work at the age of nine. He dropped out of school in the 10th grade. At present, only the youngest child, a girl, has a chance to finish high school, the first and only person in the family to do so. For a time he enrolled in an adult education program in Starr County where he could earn some money while learning, but he had to leave to join the harvest.

Now Amador's chances are dwindling. Perhaps he'll fix his pickup or find another job, or he may have to leave his family, join a single men's group to hunt work in the Great Lakes area or even in Chicago where he lost a finger last year in a potato packing plant. He was an early member of the *huelga*, the strike in Starr County which pitted the No. 2 local of the UFWOC against the large farm employers along the Río Grande. If he happens to get a job in south Texas now, Amador believes, he would be out of a job as soon as the employer learned about his union activities. But he asserts that it had been a lack of education that made his parents think that earning $13 a day or less in the fields was enough. "We think differently now," he says. "We have to work together and defend ourselves to better ourselves."

The persistent pressure exerted by the need for work had enveloped Amador. It appeared, too, in the dry, matter-of-fact words of an old man wielding a hoe in a jalapeño field for $1 an hour: "If we leave now, the children won't learn anything, and they'll end up here." The time was toward the end of May, school was almost over, and many families were already gone, or waiting till the last school bell rang. Their homes would be left, boarded up, at the mercy of weather or anyone who might break in, take what little might be there. Forces pulled at them, pressing them into the stream. Yet, a chunky farm worker could still look ahead as he slapped on a thin coat of white paint to protect the clapboard sides of his home. The next night, as soon as he could sign up with the Farm Labor Service in McAllen, he would be on his way.

Beyond the vagaries of weather and timing, the south Texas Mexican American, who makes up a good part of the 103,000 persons of Spanish-surname who migrate for work, must contend with the presence of the green-carder, not by the tens, or hundreds, but by the thousands.

The border crossing at McAllen-Reynosa, one of the major crossings in the area, teems with people from Mexico, dressed for field work, of all ages and sizes, male and female. The people come to work in the U.S. because wages are higher than in Mexico and since the American dollar is worth more in pesos, it is extremely beneficial for a Mexican to obtain a greencard and work on this side during the day, returning to his home in Mexico at night.

Yet, annual income per capita in Starr County, for example, is about $1,500, and according to the report, Hunger, U.S.A., by the Citizens Board of Inquiry into Hunger and Malnutrition in the U.S., Starr County's percentage of poor families was 71.4 and its newborn death rate was at 9.7 per 1,000 in comparison to the national rate of 5.9 per 1,000. There is also evidence of greater numbers of illegal entrants into the U.S. Notably since the termination of Public Law 78 (the "bracero" program), the number of

Mexicans deported for illegal entry increased to 14,248 in 1965, nearly half again the number that had been deported just the year before, and was up to 24,385 in 1966. The actual number of illegal workers is difficult to gauge but it is possible to surmise a total twice the 1966 figure of those who are not caught.

Of major importance in evaluating the impact of the greencarder is that apart from the loss of jobs to resident workers and the suppression of wages, the situation forces upwards of 75 percent of the Mexican American population out of the area to find work. The migrant is thus deprived of opportunities in education, job training, housing, and the exercise of certain civil rights. As long as he must leave home for three to six months of the year, he cannot build a sound and solid base of political and social involvement in his home community. The Colonias del Valle, however, point toward a method by which the migrant can maintain an organization from which will flow the kinds of activities and services other regions take for granted. Ed Krueger, a United Church of Christ minister doing non-denominational work in the valley since 1966, has been like the rock fallen into the stream which little by little catches branches floating down willy-nilly until an island, even a dam is formed. Twenty colonias have formed self-help committees since October 1967. In turn, the colonias have set up a joint council to work on common problems. It is still too early to become too enthusiastic about the colonias' organizing efforts, Krueger said, and summer will be the first major test of the new movement.

There are signs in Starr County that things are changing for the better, he added. For example, a coalition of the poor people, the United Farm Workers local in Río Grande City, led by Gil Padilla, national vice president of the union, and some teachers and businessmen concerned with the conduct of government, ousted several county officials and elected two people to the school board in the May primary elections.

A coalition like this has never succeeded before in south Texas; the current efforts may fail, or be long in making changes but a new start has been made in which the farm worker himself is crucially involved. A colonia leader, who had a large family and who could ill afford to migrate, said: "We are fighting for the children. We must keep faith in one another—that is what counts. We face indifference every day here but even though we've never united before, we know that this is the only way to change our children's future."

The highways of the migrant stream inevitably lead back to the legislative and administrative problems which slow progress or block change for the itinerant farm worker. A detailed and comprehensive program which would affect most phases of the farm worker's life is set forth in the February 1968 Report (No. 1006) of the Senate Subcommittee on Migratory Labor of the Committee on Labor and Public Welfare. Suggestions for revisions or provisions in the law dealing with collective bargaining rights, foreign workers, voluntary farm employment service, unemployment insurance, workmen's compensation, old age, survivors, and disability insurance, residence requirements for public assistance and for voting eligibility, and for a National Advisory Council on Migratory Labor—all of these basic factors—are covered by the Senate Report.

From the evidence in Delano and south Texas, perhaps in the future for the Garden State, the migrant farm worker may yet obtain the essence of the American dream: self-determination through personal participation in the forces which shape our lives. He will have to do this in spite of the indifference and resistance of certain sections of society, but he is becoming more aware that he can achieve a measure of dignity through his own efforts. The migrants, one realizes, are among the most oppressed and disadvantaged people in America. On the other hand, their economic deprivation could be the easiest problem to resolve. How a man can be brought back to self-respect, self-confidence, is another thing. Perhaps, it is only through unionization and community organization that this is possible. As long as inequities of law and practice persist, farm workers will continue to be denied rights and opportunities even while other groups are achieving them. They simply will not have the choice to stay on or to abandon those highways of misery.

ENRIQUETA LONGAUEX Y VÁSQUEZ

The Woman of La Raza

While attending a Mexican-American conference in Colorado this year, I went to one of the workshops that were held to discuss the role of the Chicana—the Mexican-American woman, the woman of La Raza. When the time came for the women to report to the full conference, the only thing that the workshop representative had to say was this: "It was the consensus of the group that the Chicana woman does not want to be liberated."

As a woman who has been faced with living as a member of the Mexican-American minority group, as a breadwinner and a mother raising children, living in housing projects, and having much concern for other humans plus much community involvement, I felt this as quite a blow. I could have cried. Surely we could at least have come up with something to add to that statement. I sat back and thought, Why? Why? Then I understood why the

Originally published as "The Mexican American Woman," in Robin Morgan, ed., *Sisterhood Is Powerful* (New York: Random House, 1970). Reprinted by permission of Enriqueta Longauex y Vásquez. The notes are the editors'.

statement had been made and I realized that going along with the feelings of the men at the convention was perhaps the best thing to do at the time.

Looking at the history of the Chicana or Mexican woman, we see that her role has been a very strong one—although a silent one. When the woman has seen the suffering of her people, she has always responded bravely and as a totally committed and equal human. My mother told me of how, during the time of Pancho Villa and the revolution in Mexico, she saw the men march through the village continually for three days and then she saw the battalion of women marching for a whole day. The women carried food and supplies; also, they were fully armed and wearing loaded *Carrilleras.*[1] In battle, they fought alongside the men. Out of the Mexican Revolution came the revolutionary personage "Adelita," who wore her *rebozo*[2] crossed at the bosom as a symbol of the revolutionary women in Mexico.

Then we have our heroine Juana Gallo, a brave woman who led her men to battle against the government after having seen her father and other villagers hung for defending the land of the people. She and many other women fought bravely with their people. And if called upon again, they would be there alongside the men to fight to the bitter end.

Today, as we hear the call of La Raza and as the dormant, "docile," Mexican-American comes to life, we see again the stirring of the people. With that call, the Chicana woman also stirs and I am sure that she will leave her mark upon the Mexican-American movement in the Southwest.

How the Chicana woman reacts depends totally on how the *macho*[3] Chicano is treated when he goes out into the "mainstream of society." If the husband is so-called successful, the woman seems to become very domineering and demands more and more in material goods. I ask myself at times, Why are the women so demanding? Can they not see what they make of their men? But then I realize: this is the price of owning a slave.

A woman who has no way of expressing herself and of realizing herself as a full human has nothing else to turn to but the owning of material things. She builds her entire life around these, and finds security in this way. All she has to live for is her house and family; she becomes very possessive of both. This makes her a totally dependent human. Dependent on her husband and family. Most of the Chicana women in this comfortable situation are not particularly involved in the movement. Many times it is because of the fear of censorship in general. Censorship from the husband, the family, friends, and society in general. For these reasons she is completely inactive.

Then you will find the Chicana whose husband was not able to fare so very well in society, and perhaps has had to face defeat. This is the Chicana who really suffers. Quite often the man will not fight the real source of his problems, be it discrimination or whatever, but will instead come home and

[1]gun belts   [2]shawl   [3]supermasculine

take it out on his family. As this continues, his Chicana becomes the victim of his *machismo* and woeful are the trials and tribulations of that household.

Much of this is seen, particularly in the city. The man, being head of the household but unable to fight the System he lives in, will very likely lose face and for this reason there will often be a separation or divorce in a family. It is at this time that the Chicana faces the real test of having to confront society as one of its total victims.

There are many things she must do. She must: 1) find a way to feed and clothe the family; 2) find housing; 3) find employment; 4) provide child care; and 5) find some kind of social outlet and friendship.

1) In order to find a way to feed and clothe her family, she must find a job. Because of her suppression she has probably not been able to develop a skill. She is probably unable to find a job that will pay her a decent wage. If she is able to find a job at all, it will probably be sought only for survival. Thus she can hope just to exist; she will hardly be able to live an enjoyable life. Here one of the most difficult problems for the Chicana woman to face is that of going to work. Even if she does have a skill, she must all at once realize that she has been living in a racist society. She will have much difficulty in proving herself in any position. Her work must be three times as good as that of the Anglo majority. Not only this, but the competitive way of the Anglo will always be there. The Anglo woman is always there with her superiority complex. The Chicana woman will be looked upon as having to prove herself even in the smallest task. She is constantly being put to the test. Not only does she suffer the oppression that the Anglo woman suffers as a woman in the market of humanity, but she must also suffer the oppression of being a minority person with a different set of values. Because her existence and the livelihood of the children depend on her conforming, she tries very hard to conform. Thus she may find herself even rejecting herself as a Mexican-American. Existence itself depends on this.

2) She must find housing that she will be able to afford. She will very likely be unable to live in a decent place; it will be more the matter of finding a place that is cheap. It is likely that she will have to live in a housing project. Here she will be faced with the real problem of trying to raise children in an environment that is conducive to much suffering. The decision as to where she will live is a difficult matter, as she must come face-to-face with making decisions entirely on her own. This, plus having to live them out, is very traumatic for her.

3) In finding a job she will be faced with working very hard during the day and coming home to an empty house and again having to work at home. Cooking, washing, ironing, mending, plus spending some time with the children. Her role changes to being both father and mother. All of this, plus being poor, is very hard to bear. On top of this, to have a survey worker or

social worker tell you that you have to have incentive and motivations—these are tough pressures to live under. Few men could stand up under such pressures.

4) Child care is one of the most difficult problems for a woman to have to face alone. Not only is she tormented with having to leave the raising of her children to someone else, but she wants the best of care for them. For the amount of money that she may be able to pay from her meager wages, it is likely that she will be lucky to find anyone at all to take care of the children. The routine of the household is not normal at all. She must start her day earlier than an average worker. She must clothe and feed the children before she takes them to be cared for in someone else's home. Then too, she will have a very hard day at work, for she is constantly worrying about the children. If there are medical problems, this will only multiply her stress during the day. Not to mention the financial pressure of medical care.

5) With all of this, the fact still remains that she is a human and must have some kind of friendship and entertainment in life, and this is perhaps one of the most difficult tasks facing the Mexican-American woman alone. She can probably enjoy very little entertainment, since she can not afford a babysitter. This, plus the fact that she very likely does not have the clothes, transportation, etc. As she cannot afford entertainment herself, she may very often fall prey to letting someone else pay for her entertainment and this may create unwanted involvement with some friend. When she begins to keep company with men, she will meet with the disapproval of her family and often be looked upon as having loose moral values. As quite often she is not free to remarry in the eyes of the Church, she will find more and more conflict and disapproval, and she continues to look upon herself with guilt and censorship. Thus she suffers much as a human. Everywhere she looks she seems to be rejected.

This woman has much to offer the movement of the Mexican-American. She has had to live all of the roles of her Raza. She has had to suffer the torments of her people in that she has had to go out into a racist society and be a provider as well as a mother. She has been doubly oppressed and is trying very hard to find a place. Because of all this, she is a very, very strong individual. She has had to become strong in order to exist against these odds.

The Mexican-American movement is not that of just adults fighting the social system, but it is a total commitment of a family unit living what it believes to be a better way of life in demanding social change for the benefit of humankind. When a family is involved in a human rights movement, as is the Mexican-American family, there is little room for a woman's liberation movement alone. There is little room for having a definition of woman's role as such. Roles are for actors and the business at hand requires people living the examples of social change. The Mexican-American-movement demands are such that, with the liberation of La Raza, we must have a total liberation. The woman must help liberate the man and the man must look upon this liberation with the woman at his side, not behind him, following, but alongside of him, leading. The family must come up together.

The Raza movement is based on brother- and sisterhood. We must look at each other as one large family. We must look at all of the children as belonging to all of us. We must strive for the fulfillment of all as equals, with the full capability and right to develop as humans. When a man can look upon a woman as human, then, and only then, can he feel the true meaning of liberation and equality.

Poetry

LEONARD ADAMÉ

Lost Together with Our Children

In the barber shop
      I see your ebony face
      against fluorescent lights
      black pebble eyes
looking down
      your clubfoot

boot wax on your hands
they read old newspapers
      afraid of
      your touching
      even their shoes.

We look into our eyes
not speaking
      we smile
      a little
      we know
      of each other
      and

of our accents
      lost together
      with our children
      crying in
      the playground
not wanting to
      come home.

On Sides of Tractor Paths

In the shed
showing me
nailing, stacking
of cherry tomato lugs.

Talking softly,
only of nailing,
hearing you through
the hum of machine noise.

Your eyes wide,
stepping on the pedal
releasing 300 pounds
of pressure

hundreds of times,
every day,
eyes unchanging,
wide and quiet and brown.

Lunch alone by
the nailer, tacos
dripping chile colorado
from a grease-stained
lunch bag.

At 5:00 waiting,
your wife in the field,
children asleep in
the new rusty '50 Chevy.

June, then suddenly August,
sweat and overripe fruit
rotting on sides
of tractor paths.

One day, another at
the machine,
familiar rhythm broken.

When I asked, someone said
in the field
while they irrigated
you shot your rifle
at the foreman, your eyes wide,
he running through vines
screaming.

Then, your wife looking,
the barrel to your mouth,
you shot again.

In the payroll line
they put $1.65 in
mud-stained pockets
and did not stay
to laugh and talk
as on other days.

ERNESTO TREJO

Chac

For Tara

I am Chac
I bring rain upon my people
because of me their corn grows
because of me, Chac,
they are ancient
they are eternal
the Mayas

the promised child is missing
among my people
          (I hear voices whispering
          We Are With The Pope as
          someone cries, the hills
          are naked, the sky is silent,
          a dirty look calls for death,
          corn hardly grows now)

life is not complete, we are not complete

a long time ago
before there was light
—and Mayas—
I was sad:
out of my tears cenotes[1] formed.
My children, the Mayas,
cycles later, chanted to me,
for I dwell in their hearts
      (I am hungry, I am weak,
      there is no corn).

I hear you now Mayas
keep chanting, fight in my name
we shall meet again
in Chichén-Itzá
your chants feed my stomach
saturate my blood
fill my throat, my lungs
touch my soul
life seems dead,
unreal,
but you are eternal
Mayas, people of the Sun
for Chac is with you
        forever.

To Brothers Dead Crossing the Rápido River . . . 194 . . .

in a day
      in an afternoon
           in a night
                 in years of fury
and tears
      alone and far from home
               away from familiar sounds
                      tender arms

[1]deposits of water found in Mexico generally at a great depth; believed to be places of sacrifice in some areas

you fell on the earth of Italy
                    blood of Mexico
                              blood of the northern
                                             deserts
blood of the bitter border
                    spilled on the earth of Italy
on the earth of Italy
hope of america
              the vain hope of america
                                never realized hope of america
against a wall of teuton steel
                    you waded the chilling river
                                        water tasting of
                                                    death
far from home
              tasting of sudden death
                              left your dead on the river banks
tears of mothers on the river banks

LUIS OMAR SALINAS

Tihuitkli

Tihuitkli[1]
        you slew the python
then went off
on your motorcycle
            to buy a hamburger/
and nobody gave a damn
not even your grandmother
who raised you/
and now we see you
with your girl friends
talking about Plato
                and Kafka
wearing Levis
and going to movie houses/

[1]Indian name

Tihuitkli
        you're welcome
                    here
but what are your
                    people
going to say
when they see you
singing
        American songs
to the village girls?

Popocatepetl

I

Popocatepetl[1]
        you piss over the land
as night grows strong
you and your shadows
strum guitars
and I hear the songs
of spiders
        becoming human
with the earth
as they lead their
        armies
to a brutal death/
What great prince
nursed and gave you wisdom
kissing the nipple
of adventure
        and rivalry/

II

Oh Popocatepetl
        your girls
are turning hippie

[1]a volcano in Mexico

in your dark avenues
their vigorousness
                    waking
the forests
and Indians going
                    to burials/

III

Popocatepetl
        young men
are going crazy
in the graveyards
and in the fields
            where roses
        lose their blood
                    daily/
        new battlefields
for Aztec gods/

IV

Popocatepetl
        look how your seeds
flow over the land
        mating with the çorn
tearing loose
the earth
            from familiar hands/

V

Those hands
that tried to cover
you with rain prayers
                and pollen
        in the sacrificial temple
                    of Wescotlipi/[2]

---

[2]Virgin girls were reputedly sacrificed here.

VI

Oh Popocatepetl
    your cries of rape
and plunder
  are still
heard in the village/
and when your tears
become too much for you
you sing
       defeated
submissive
angel-like Popocatepetl/

Mestizo

I

We have walked for miles
Without water or food to your church
America
      how about getting us a bus
and some food and water
or we'll burn the
        church down

II

In the fields
   and in the barrios
our
   Mestizos
are fed up with conditions/
and we believe
in our man from Delano
    César Chávez
because the rich man
has put us down
    for many years/
so when you hear Huelga
watch it
     'cause we're on our way/

III

In the fields
and in the barrios
            Mestizos
are singing songs

IV

Let's help our Mestizos
            America
It's about time
No?

V

Our color is brown
our blood
            comes from the Spanish
the Aztec
and the Mayan
      we had a great empire once
            we are rich in tradition
and we know what it is to suffer.

Guevara . . . Guevara

Guevara . . . Guevara
   we have come to claim your body
            undertakers of a huge America
cutting through shrubs of a
                        silent heaven
            saddened
   by your blood that flows from
            darkened leaves
         on the Bolivian hills

we plunder through the world
                  in search of you

and find you
a child
passionate and hungry
(the passion of your mother Ché)
your eyes form avenues
for dusty withered skulls
through grass
blood
and more blood

Guevara . . . Guevara wake up
it is raining in Bolivia
and the campesinos
with voices of lead
are talking with putrid suspicion
(sinews and flesh from Argentina Ché)

and secretive Gods with sharpened axes
look for your body
as cocaine
smolders
from the windows
making disguises
in the huge Bolivian sky
(the landing Ché . . . the landing)
Guevara . . . Guevara
there is hunger in Bolivia
and children mumble on the hilltops
with your lips
(the river is strewn with dead communists
Guevara)

and that mystery that talks of you
on that damp earth
waiting for that troubled sea
to chant
Guevara . . . Guevara
we have found you
your blood fills our throats
our lungs
our belly
with a smell as fresh
as yesterday's fallen snow

Señor Torres

Señor Torres
You know
      I am Mestizo
and that I am poor/

why do you
cheat
    us
in the weighing
of our cotton?

Hasn't Choucuatl
told you
we planned
to kill you?

Your blood
on our
      cotton
will make
beautiful blankets.

ROBERTO ENRIQUE VARGAS

They Blamed It on Reds

Vincent Gutíerrez died
At the hands of mercenaries
In the mission on Mother's Day.
The people rose together and
Marched at his funeral procession
Beginning at St. Peter's Church
Down 24th St. to South Van Ness St.
Finally boarding the following cars
And driving the rest of the way
To Holy Cross Cemetery, Colma
Thursday May 14th Aztlán/Babylon

I

Thursday . . . crying . . . St. Peter's church . . . organ
Incense . . . lágrimas[1] . . . 10:30 morning . . . sun/hot
Faces . . . old/young . . . Vincent gone
Anger/love . . . Chente[2] gone now
Eunuch chronicles plastered with lies
Reds, Reds melting in American minds
Brought to you in living color by CBS
Dial soap and the puppet-coroners
of the TV world . . .

II

Tears (saladas)[3] . . . dry lips
Black hearse yawns/swallows
18 years of Chente . . . gone
Not killed in Cambodia . . . but war
(Padre nuestro que está en los[4] . . .)
Walking now . . . the last 24th St.
Business as usual . . . slower
Hundreds of sisters/brothers
Following behind/in you
Angered in love walking
Past walls of cornucopia
Solid-lined by Pig-nalgas[5]
7-up signs gleaming
Sears . . . Bank of America
Old Glory still . . . stop/go.
Madre[6]/Hija[7]/Esposa[8] . . . crying
Llantos . . . stop/go
Chente en el medio de Mayo[9]
Gone!
And the priest raises the chalice
("This is my body This is my blood")

III

South Van Ness red light
In cars now pollution (F–310)

---

[1]tears   [2]Vincent   [3]salty   [4]Our Father who art in   [5]asses   [6]Mother
[7]Daughter   [8]Wife   [9]Vincent in the middle of May

Firestone Rent-a-Limousine . . . stop/go
The mechanical centipede slowed
By Progress   stop/go
        Business as usual
"¡Hijo, hijo . . . te han asesinado!"[10]
I just tapped him across the . . .
It seems an overdose of . . .
Business as usual . . . stop/go

IV

Look back
Look back Chente . . . si puedes[11]
Remember the Roach Pad hunger
Joys . . . highs, sorrows?
Mission sidewalks (BART raped)
Hum goodbye pa' siempre carnal[12]
But the genocide trail begins su fin[13]
Trembling with the weight of our guns . . ./
Chente 18 brown and dead
In the land of E Pluribus Unum
Dead in the land of the Apollos/
Edsel . . . Titanic . . . U2 and Gary Powers
Mission Hi . . . State College
        and business as usual/

V

Now passing local draft board
Vision of monsoon flies
Bloodsmell cheeks of bronze
Organisms shell-pierced screams of death
Vietnam! Vietnam!
        Chente dies everywhere
        (Blame the reds!)
En los barrios de Guatemala[14]
San Francisco or Mississippi
        (Blame the reds!)

[10]Son, son . . . they have assassinated you   [11]if you can   [12]forever brother
[13]its end   [14]In the *barrios* of Guatemala

VI

Holy Cross . . . silent in wait
Lágrimas de madre[15] soak black lace
　　Hijo. Hijo no te vayas[16]
　　　Wife wails ripped/soul fright
　　　　　　alone now . . .
Chente flows into open wound
In earth . . . magic dance of
Mayan ancestors . . . tears
Silent war drums sound
Chente killed by the Guardians
　　　　　　of Enterprise
Their red white and blue
phallic symbols thrust deep
　　　　　　in our throats . . .
Moist dirt falls . . . covers
Ashes to ashes . . . peace brother
Peace . . .　　　business as usual

"Blame it on reds!"

Elegy Pa Gringolandia in 13 Cantos

It seems . . . just the other day
Acid/Guru/Dr Leary tuned into his local Weathermen
Turned on to a million micrograms of Marx
And dropped out of Apathy (Tune in
　　　　　　　Turn on
　　　　　　　　　Drop out?)

It seems . . . just the other day
Brother Hendrix Dreamt
Of Decibels . . . Glowing ebony
holes in the air-Nirvahna (and the wind
　　　　　　　　cries
　　　　　　　　　Mary . . .)

[15]Tears of a mother   [16]Son. Son don't go

It seems . . . just the other day
Sister Angela's car was found, raped
sentenced . . . to hang
Buried at San Jose State
By 10 most wanted allmale Elks Club
Card carrying (FBI) Klansmen (Keep on Runnin
                              Keep on Hidin)

It seems . . . just the other day
Fidel sang: "Tumba la caña[1]
Jivarito Túmbala"[2] and prayed often in silence
For the love of our people (Zafra
                              Zafra)

It seems . . . just the other day
80 Arabs and 1 Nicaraguan said
"This is the only way to fly"
We'll take 4 (Hallah leila
                  Hallah)

It seems . . . just the other day
Fire/Brimstone MacIntyre assucked
Saigon's Cowed Coa Ky to come
make war here Rally Round
The Flag boys—from the halls
Of Montezooma (Column
                  Right
                  Ho)

It seems . . . just the other day
5 L.A. Puercos[3] left
2 Mejicano[4] Brothers' lives . . . fading
Into the also fading linoleum and history
Because they all look alike
And spoke no English (Basta Ya![5]
                  Basta Ya!)

[1]Knock down the cane   [2]Jivarito Knock it down   [3]Pigs
[4]Mexican   [5]Enough Now

It seems . . . just the other day
6 million Chicanos offed their cactus
And cried chale[6] no we won't go
The Álamo is alive and falling
In L.A. Remember the Salazars
And Chente . . . (Chicano Power
                    Chicano Power)

It seems . . . just the other day
Los Siete[7] played Latino[8] musical chairs
all the witnesses in Amerikka
(Bound by oath) Hollered! Desafinado!
They all look alike
Maybe They're from L.A.
While my brothers mambo softly
In their minds/Mambo, Qué Rico[9] El Mambo/(Free los 7
                                              Free los 7)

It seems . . . just the other day
Brother Victor Cruz changed his
Channel . . . again . . . took another sip
Of his Margarita sucked smoke
From fine cigar and sang Poems
For liberation (Papo got
                    his
                gun
                SNAP!)

It seems . . . just the other day
Mohawk brave Oakes packed
Wife/child/friends into beat up
Silver Buffalo . . . bus to rediscover Life
Squaw teepees feathers y Indo-América (Alcatraz lives
                                          no
                                    Birdman)

[6]hell   [7]The Seven   [8]Latin   [9]how pleasing the mambo is